THE GREAT ESCAPE

Donald Gorbach

ISBN-10 1979687803
ISBN-13 978-1979687805

"YOU KNOW, TO MARRY A MAN LIKE DONALD, YOU NEED TO KNOW WHO YOU ARE, AND YOU NEED TO BE VERY STRONG AND SMART… I'M NOT A 'YES' PERSON. NO MATTER WHO YOU ARE MARRIED TO, YOU STILL NEED TO LEAD YOUR LIFE."

— MELANIA TRUMP

REALITYCOVERBOOKS.COM